Gods and Devils in Leyton

Michael Clements

PublishAmerica
Baltimore

First printing

ISBN: 1-4241-0616-8
PUBLISHED BY PUBLISHAMERICA, LLLP
www.publishamerica.com
Baltimore

Printed in the United States of America

This book is dedicated to

Grabielle, Kirk and Karn,

feared on the street as Pirate, Asbo and Tea Leaf

(and not forgetting Bridget and Joseph)

Table of Contents

Valley of the Kings, an Invocation

Her presence fills all that parched
landscape of jagged ravines
and bare buttresses
of crimson, purple and tawny rock,
and the chasms fill
with flowers, and her breath
is a cool mist upon desolation.
She is Egypt's one true love,
black, powerful and immortal,
older than the *djinn*, born
not from fire but from the Will of Atum;
sister to the night sky,
mother of the avenging hawk
and guardian of the Key of Life,
crossing the blue waters
to Cyprus and Athens
where her star-clad twin
has stepped forth
from the divine brow of mighty Zeus.

Invitation

You have been selected at random as the recipient
of a major prize. It involves a romantic
journey to Old Mexico, where you will spend
one night in a secret chamber
on top of the Pyramid of the Sun in downtown Teotihuacan,
and an eternity in heaven with Coatlicue (the Snake Lady).
Unclothed maidens will give you
peyote and chocolate, then strap you down
on a bloodstained basalt stone,
while a tittering old fool in a mask dances
around waving a knife of black volcanic glass.

This is an adventure holiday
and the experience of a (shortened) lifetime.
Regretfully, we do not provide travel
or medical insurance, though the masked priest
has wide experience in trauma counselling.

Should you decline the invitation, a very motivated
Coatlicue will insist on crossing the Poison Water
for a face-to-face interview, probably at midnight,
by a crossroads, when you are totally alone.
(She takes her marketing responsibilities very seriously,
and has received three medals from the Minister of Tourism).

—Your ritual transfiguration will be the same,
though she may insist on a cross-species organ transplant as well,
to help you fit in with the other damned souls and nightstalkers, as
there can be no reservation in paradise for those who reject this
ultimate honour offered so generously by our proud beauty.

Of course, you will miss out on the exotic dancers
and the mind-expanding drugs
if you reject this amazing offer, and I can only suggest

that having your beating heart ripped out on a warm
tropical night is preferable to dismemberment
at the hands of an angry lady
in a damp corner of Epping Forest.

Motor-Cycle Pie

"I have been grinding out strange airs
on the organs of old Amsterdam,"
mused the Great God Pan,
astride his motor-cycle of violence,
"and now I am back with a vengeance."

He blocked my way with folded arms:
"And with this *Harley*
I shall bring you to parlay!"

"Please," I began, "I have Papa Legba
installed in my front room,
ordering *balti* and *döner kebabs,*
and phoning the family in Port-au-Prince,
Aphrodite in a naughty nightie
sleeping in my bath—and not to mention
Castor & Pollux dead drunk in each other's arms,
so save the rhyming charms—
I don't fancy any more divinities
hanging around and taking liberties."

"But I need somewhere to crash (metaphorically)
during the cosmic makeover,
and I must presume upon our shared nationality."
(For I was born in Hell though chose to be a refugee.)

So it was, I had him, cleaning motor-cycle pieces
in my kitchen, adding to the argument divine
over "this is my toothbrush and not thine!"
or the sacred hands snatching for the remote,
for the gods cannot agree about the BBC
and pester me to pay the devil for Sky.

The Elder Tree

I found the philosopher's stone hidden
in an elderberry and a sly toad
hopped from a hole in the roots where I stood,
not changing into the princess I'd summoned.
Only a girl clad in grey-green leather
with earrings dangling, and goggling amber
eyes, gazed at me witless, then ran away,
croaking indignantly, occasionally leaping.
Frowning, I polished the stone on my sleeve
and my shirt became cloth of gold.

I went to the cemetery and tried
to raise the dead, but not even Cornelius
Agrippa took notice. I rubbed the stone on
a marble angel and it turned into
a robot from Japan, all chrome and rubber,
which followed me about, babbling and sparking:
"Chotto motte kudasai !" Luckily
the lurking toad-girl jumped him in the bushes.

I had one last try in the supermarket,
turned slimming wafers into human flesh
and bottles of table wine into blood,
which then exploded, as Scripture warns us.
—The quest for magical enlightenment
is a sorry thing indeed for mystics
within the suburban environment.

This stone, rarer than the basilisk's eye,
master of transformations, now grew dim,
leaving me with a disco-dancer's shirt
and a fly-catching stalker and her sweet.
(The bloody supermarket was closed by
public health, after an outcry, forcing
us all to take the bus to make ends meet.)

Shagga Rag at Carnival

Do the witch dance of Jiggery Pokery in the dark,
while the wheel in your head spins around
and around and wave your weaving shagga stick
at the sweatery shadows who surround.
Men with painted faces will overturn
the festooned night and many women will sing
abandoned along the rain-slicked streets.

I have letters patent from Babalu with His Great Seal
and may shake my knees in every gutter
and kick up the banana skins and orange peel
and jigger and poker, grimace and splutter,
to the tremendous music of the Carnival Wheel
outside the Jaggery Mart where they bag the sweets
with red-rimmed eyes and twitch and turn.

Twitch and turn, for there's a bogey-man about,
in a coat of blue and kickery boots,
who wants to dance on the children's heads
and beat a tune with his morningstar cane:
but Shagga Jag will blow dust in his eyes
and choke his throat and piggery snout
and lead him a dance down a snickery lane.

Even the dead dance out of their unconsecrated beds
when Shagga shakes his painted staff,
and the worlds open up like a pack of cards
offering our souls rebirth and jig-a-jig pleasures,
and in our dancing we leap and laugh
from painted image to the next in timeless measures.

A Prayer for the Animation of Buildings

Mother of mysteries liberate poor Merlin
from that dimensionless, lightless and lost oak.
Listen to this plea, that London might yet be free
of Mammon and his monuments, and all those who
grovel at his clay feet: especially bankers.

Look at the map of their City—you will see
a strange pattern emerging of lines, squares,
circles, pentacles and mystic sextiles,
sited on old churches, ancient mounds, graves
and Mithraica. Keep on looking, find
the underlying blueprint: Stock Exchange
to Bank to St Alphage, a right-angled
triangle, enclosing St Margaret
Lothbury, another Wren curio:
and an excellent start for our rough art.

Traffic-flow, you know, is part of it, noise
muffled by narrow streets but directed upward
like puritan hymns in those lightless, grim
churches: but a better effect comes from long
processions on holy days—the ancient
Chaldaeans knew the craft well—and we should
make use of the Shagga Jag Carnival,
and its stone-breaking, pigeon-plummeting,
foundations-flaying, black hole of jittery-jolly
NOISE.

With one grand rattle may their City
tear loose from its steel and concrete stanchions
and float away past Wanstead Flats leaving
a pit abysmal, empty of the diabolical throne.

Then may Bran return home, Lord of Lightful
Things, and make fruitful bowers of these sad,

demonic temples. So might the maidens
make again the mad May dance, toss flowers out of doors
for heroes to catch, and make us forget
false accounting, convenient lies and profitable wars.

Farewell, you sons of bitches, usurers and lackies
of brummagem riches as your square mile goes astray
into the mud of the estuary somewhere near
Gravesend and becomes a clay Pompeii.

Master of the Lightning

You may wake me from sleep,
calling on the cold north wind,
but I do not fear for teeth in the dark
and my shabby pillow of ferns
holds my spirit steady in dream.
Some days I can feast on cheesecake,
and others keep holy by fasting,
and some days can trudge many miles
and others dedicate to meditation.
Many are envious of this pilgrimage,
hating their mired lives,
and curse me when I dance to the slow
music of the Pleiades, but being
a seventh son of Mother Earth,
I am Master of the Lightning
and can read whole histories
in the charred stumps of trees,
and find nuggets of gold
turned up by the thunderbolt.

Calypso & Co

Spinning up like a top, the wicked old witch
showered me with broken brown leaves
from the gutter, then leaped upon my front wall,
croaking this curse from chapped lips :

May you turn a familiar corner and
be jumped and publicly degraded
in broad daylight by a leather-clad feminist
motor-cycle gang on speed.

Crouching down and cackling,
she produced a column of termites
from her dried prune mouth.
These encircled the chestnut tree outside my gate
and began to devour it, leaving behind a hollow trunk
full of white wood shavings. She added :

May you win a telephone prize
and your aging cruise ship
run aground on the Skeleton Coast
while you watch the crew make off
in the only seaworthy lifeboat.

Before the ill-omened hag could add
a further verse to her rotten curse,
the dark clouds parted and we saw within a rainbow:
Athena's 737 from Corfu on its way to Stansted.
"Oops!" she said, "bad timing! Your lodger is back."
and turned into a haughty black-haired girl
in a red and gold *peplos*. "Very well."
I sighed: "You can move into the cellar,
but I have promised space to Circe
and Sycorax and you will have to
sling a hammock each between the beams."

Circe wanted to keep pigs in the back garden,
and I had to agree as she alone could restore the tree,
and send the termites packing. In this way, the Magical Three
began their nightclub career combining
hypnotism and illusions with stand-up comedy.

Immortal

Cast off this shadow and soar:
tell unkind Death that I have left
and am unobtainable, for I ride
dragons astride in the purple evening.
See below, my castle is prepared for me,
the candles are all lit for guests
and my servants have prepared
a solemn banquet. I have drunk
from the cup of Holy Wisdom
and now I can move the lightning
with my shoulder and turn red
pillar-boxes like prayer wheels.
So drink your rum for Baron Samedi.
There is no double-entry bookkeeping
in my dukedom and I have banished
the bogey-men beyond the black stump
and the Great White Stone:
stroll through this art gallery and museum
of eternity as a tourist, but always
behave with the self-assurance
of a born resident, and smoke your cigar

Bad Poets

Philip Larkin would hammer your bowler hat down
over your ears with flying fists if you returned
your loan books late, and Emily Dickinson too spurned
fines in favour of a kicking all around the town.
Others were no better: I once saw Gerard Manley Hopkins
and G.K. Chesterton chase Friedrich Nietzsche for three blocks
because he pronounced "Gott ist tot!" at a church bazaar.
Alfred Lord Tennyson would drop-kick you in the ballocks
if you mentioned the name of Charles Pierre Baudelaire.
Elizabeth Barrett Browning stoned French symbolists
with rocks
in secret company with her apoplectic pa.
She shot at Paul Verlaine from behind a hedge,
missed him, but he got an almighty scare.

If you refused an OBE, Rudyard Kipling would waylay
you in a public park with garden shears
and snip off both your ears,
but if you voted Tory, Byron would cut you dead
in the street, Shelley would bomb your carriage, and Keats
would scrawl *PIG* on your front door with a whitewash brush.
Chaucer regularly hurled critics of his verses
under loaded cheese waggons uttering the filthiest curses;
a sozzled Goethe pinched girls' behinds
in big department stores,
and inevitably earned himself a well-deserved bum's rush.

By far the worst was that government stooge,
Wordsworth, the cur,
who would get the Yeomanry to hold you down on a stove
while he applied with funnel and tube a nitric acid enema.
"Confess!" he'd shriek, "I want those names,
you Bonapartist freak!"
and have them shovel more Hanoverian coal on the fire.

Walt Whitman and Christina Rosetti wrestled tigers
in the circus for gin-money and when it was all spent,
formed a masked gang and stuck up three banks in Hove.
So you see, no real artist ever did relent a life of crime
and colour, or tire
of unseemly brawling and rebellious antiphons
but whether sour librarian or heroic gent, their biographers
hide the dirty linen in the closet with the skeletons.

The Transfiguration on the Mountain

I have climbed the high hill from *The Green Man*
and watched the Blind Man fighting
with the scarecrow in the fields below me:
his fists move like pistons on the empty
air, and straw, not blood, is all that he spills.
Evil animates our enemies and
we are too blind to see that Old Typhon's
latest trick, as he wails over the corpse
of a victim, but we vote for him
clad in borrowed rags, the Man of Straw,
who owns half the world and rents all the rest.

It pays dividends to shop a neighbour
for New Labour, to be part of the new
refugee-free zone, to place the greenback before the euro,
to be globally
in the know, to be a new lord on a
high chair, and not taking in Poor Old Cow
slumped in a shop doorway with her bundle
cradled like a broken baby, whimpering
in her doze, remembering lost May Days.

Only May Day can get her to her feet
drunk and roaring: young again will she flounce
full of divine frenzy, dancing the step
learned in the Kent hopfields! Free for one day
from sickness and despair. The Man of Straw
pisses on derelicts in shop doorways,
spectacles all steamed up, and kicks them hard
in the head, if they lie still and don't fight back....

Once when young, she saw the vision of *Our
Lady* from the steamed-up window of a
69 bus, holding out her white arms
in supplication to the November

moon and pulled at her mother's sleeve: "Mum ! Mum !
Look at the silver lady!" Small children
can see gods, where adults see only old
newspapers and rags blowing in the wind.

The vision stuck with her and as she swam
in a Kentish pool some ten years later
with her rowdy band, all nude and glistening
like freckled Amazons, saw the silver
lady again, astride the heavens with
seven stars for a godly crown, one hand
upon the Lion, the other raised in
benediction: so that she knew that She
had marked her down for Her own.
All the years of pain and sorrow passed like rainwater
leaving her sack-slumped in that dank doorway.

In her black bundle she clutched her last link
to her lost love, the Blind Man's accordion,
pawned many times but never lost. Because
this wheezy old box was the key to re-
starting the universe. Forget the trump
of surly Gabriel on his cemetery stump,
between her breasts lay the one primal sound
of the rhyme of doing and undoing,
created by wise Merlin in the form
of an ivory extra key inscribed
with the rune *thorn* and hidden in harp
and lute until passed on to a sailor,
the seventh son of a seventh son, who
added it to his grandad's accordion.

That night, *Our Lady,* Huntress of Heaven,
appeared to Poor Old Cow for the last time.

Across from her doss an Indian girl
in a red sari waved six hands at her,
and she heard: "Go north to your lost sailor!"
Three times had *Our Lady* appeared to her
in her life, and this was the only time
she spoke. So she rose up and went eastwards
from Wardour Street, past Liverpool Street, Mile End
and Hackney through the empty streets waiting
for the Summer Solstice, and as midnight
passed, her bundle grew heavier, like an
unborn foetus quickening with his time.

Passing Whipps Cross, she rested on a bank
outside the hospital, tired, a grey-haired sack,
inconspicuous, ignored by the few
nurses and patients about, another
beggar. Ten minutes before dawn found her
on the cattle pasture looking out over
the place of the lost stone. Below
her, the Blind Man still battered the scarecrow,
while from the darkness grew shadows anew,
presaging the Longest Day. She began
to run. Through a hedge and into a field
Poor Old Cow ran gasping, her burden now
as heavy as the sins of the sleeping
continent. As she neared the warriors,
one of faint light, and one still in darkness,
the scarecrow seemed to loom above the world,
red-eyed, clawed and wicked, contemptuous
of the sailor's blows."Straw burns!" she burst out,
fumbled a match from her coat, struck it on
a stone, and set the monster ablaze. Dawn
came and with it, remembrance and new sight:
Odysseus plucked an ivory button

from his coat, bearing the rune *thorn*, meaning
GATEWAYS, and fitted it to his wheeze-box
and played the charm of undoing to set
things straight, while the Man of Straw crackled and
stank. "Penelope, my love," the sailor
said, "why do we have to keep doing this?"

An Elephant at the Disco

Dancing right hand up, left hand down
Ganesha copies his father,
the Lord of the Dance.
Heads grow out of the paving stones
and severed hands write by new life awoken:
"Satan will be free, my friends"
on the walls of the Turkish supermarket.
Blue men have been seen in Church Lane,
for Leytonstone is a centre with magickal roots
where angelic tongues are still spoken.

Summer Solstice Festival on Harrow Green
still astonishes and excites the limbs into dance,
so that we curse and leap with lolling tongues
shifting into a higher gear and more lustful.
Naked girls with crowns of myrtle
heap kisses on the sacred king
and beat him solemnly with bulrushes
while the Tattooed Man plays with his flint sickle.

I saw Death drift past on the Fire Brigade float
and he gave me a crooked smile,
passing a manicured finger over his throat:
"I still retain," he said, patting his silk twill coat,
"our agreement and your promissory note."

Above distant Canary Wharf can be spied
a plume of sacrifice from the pyramid.
Imagination is the new philosopher's stone
transmuting the history of an ancient land into
shrieking sacrifice and stained blossoms.
The Tattooed Man hacks at the prurient flesh
and we are renewed according to custom.

The Writing Is on the Wall

Better to drink export cider in the park
than to fight the dragons inside ASDA,
and to await the coming of the twilight
on a supermarket trolley of shining silver.
(A dragon falls from grace by good works
and mercy to the weak, and the ones
with name-tags are renowned in the annals of Hell.)

Barry is Jesus ! has been scrawled over
the Turkish supermarket wall,
where He turned the water into alco-pop.
The tramps in the Coronation Gardens
have passed into a morbid sleep,
without hope of resurrection by a passing creep
and there is no kiss for Lazarus.

Silenus, dozing companion of Dionysus,
lies in a puddle of piss, flies gaping,
and all he can manage for prophecy is:

What goes around, comes around.
Every other bum is a fallen angel,
and I see them hopping if not flying
to rob the shelves at the End of Daze.

Having pronounced this, he puked
into the goldfish grotto and nearly drowned.

The Fat Woman and the Tattooed Man

Herakles, that drunken dosser,
burned himself up at last
on a pile of secondhand furniture,
after killing the entire cast:
but another player who knew best,
lived on in the misty west,
faking his death with a cry to a passing ship,
now pulling faces in the demon dark,
now fathering children with a divine spark
and a smell of goat in Epping Forest.

While hunting for mistletoe bark
near the lake, a place of discarded lino,
of dying oak and flaking birch,
where old bedding and black bags surge
like an ocean over the excited rats,
I met Pan Himself, our Mayor. "I know you," He said:
"You got out and left us in the lurch."

For I was born in Hell, which is
both a place and a condition of the soul,
and exists all over this world from pole to pole,
like the singularities in Emmental cheese.
"The Fat Woman," he began to wheeze,
"has escaped again from her labyrinth
deep in Tartarus and made a beeline
for the Hollow Ponds with that swine,
an original hungry ghost, The Tattooed Man."
I reassured Himself: "The Fat Woman I know
underwent trauma therapy in Whipps Cross,
putting behind her millenia in the abused spouse role,
from a violent but sexually inadequate partner,
going down to eight stone in six and a half weeks."

"That will please her mum, Rhea, the old recluse,
but The Tattooed Man is still on the loose?"

"He does a little bare-knuckle fighting
and keeps a pit bull, drinks from the bottle, rolls his own,
and may become a political stooge some day,
being the sort of after hours fiend they breed:
a demonic bogeyman of the people,
barechested on the hunt for a fresh and frightful deed."

"We don't want his type in Hell, lowering the tone," mused Pan,
"But can I slip you something for your trouble, man?"

"I don't accept gifts from gods, or fairy gold,
dubious talents or blood-soaked IOUs,
just leave me off the electoral roll of infernal voters
and, Your Worship, we'll make our *adieus*."

Death Comes Back

Uninvited, Death came knocking on my door.
"You cut up Orpheus," I arose
and shook my fist under his nose,
"and draped the limbs over the outhouse floor,
and nailed his head to my elder tree
like a novelty Xmas decoration!
I still get funny looks from the neighbours
as a result of your wicked labours."
"Don't look at me," the beautiful god protested,
"That was the maenads, in a state of morbid excitation,
and was, in any case, his rite of passage
from street musician to universal message.

"The last time I let you go," he pursued,
"I waived the optional chess match,
and we've never seen our relationship renewed,
so can we start again from scratch?"

We sat in my bedroom, he dark browed,
compassionate and divine,
too polite to comment on the dust
to which we all return in time,
and I knew he was keen to fling his arms
about me for a possessive hug on the bed.
But I shrugged the offer of a game of chess,
and we played *Happy Families* instead.
I had to use *his* cards, of course.
Within minutes he produced *the Olympians*,
but I countered with the countless
Children of Ra. Then he tried *Mr Sky,
the Global Capitalist,* but I had all
the Sophisticated Viewers in my hand to call.

After *the Shifty Politicians* and *the Wacky Windsors*
(trumped by *the Apathetic Voters*
and *the Gutter Press Barons* to his distress)
we went down to a single card each.
His brow furrowed, and from the air
he drew *Tarot XIII, Death Himself,*
master of all living things, and gave me
an anticipatory stare.
With a sigh of resignation, but not despair,
I drew *The Lovers, Tarot VI,* for Love
conquers Death I confess.
"That's not fair!" the god exclaimed,
"only poets, mystics and children believe all that!"
"Who are you to talk of *fair*?" I said:
"Who takes the child before his time,
but leaves the bloody tyrant hale and fat?"
"Well," said the tight-lipped youth, "I've
marked your card for sure,
so expect no favours when I return for more."
Death went away muttering under his breath,
on ebon winged feet
and I must admit I heard heavenly laughter at his retreat.

Castles of Bones

There is a dragon in my pot of jam—
a little one, no doubt, but still
a creature of vast and powerful magic,
and not a newt as you insist.
No, I am pleased to buy it, but
I suggest you check your shelves
before others are planted,
by the sniggering elves.

Yes, I'll take this carton of eggs,
as three were marked by a basilisk,
together with this cornflakes packet
which has a spell from the *Lemegeton*
on the side instead of E-numbers.

Once the dead take over, things go to pot,
like *Apocalyptic Pizza* next door, where four
delivery riders lounge waiting for orders:
War always argues about his tip, brassy and bold,
Famine forgets the free garlic bread,
Pestilence coughs and sneezes over the food,
and all that Death delivers is stone cold.

I have no fears, as I'll have a pet dragon
and three cockatrice to guard my door
from unwelcome night visitors,
like that grinning clown you see
juggling lunar eggs outside the megastore.
He has too many arms, so I suggest
that walking out on this job would be best,
but first wrap my leeks in those pages
torn from the *The Revised Infernal Almagest*.

Trees Can Be Wicked Too

Our local council, sick of the Tattooed Man,
flayed him and nailed his hide
to a chestnut tree, to cure in the sun and air.
But a young girl stole his boots,
snakeskin belt, and magic ring.
Unable to make it go away
she adopted his dog on a string,
and went off whistling to the fair.

Those boots were footwear of wonder
and allowed her to open all doors
with a single kick, or to climb up
tower blocks like a gecko
while the dog barked below.
The snakeskin belt could shrink too
or marvellously grow
into a climbing rope or lasso,
and the magic ring would
make her invisible in the light of day.
But all the time the dog would bark.

Now the skin of the wicked one folded around
the trunk of the tree and his spirit possessed it:
the chestnut stood up on branch and root,
and marched off Harrow Green,
drawn by the barking in the night.
The girl, meanwhile, had a swag of loot
pilfered from some Chingford swells,
bonds and shares, a bottle of cognac,
a box of fine cheroots, and a lovely lot
of ruby clasps and diamond necklaces,
silver dollars and golden guineas
all stuffed into her gunny sack,
—and down the drainpipe she shinnies.

She was heading to her lonely squat,
halted by a cavernous pit of slack
yellow cables and leaking sewage pipes
in the middle of the *Baker's Arms* crossroads,
when the dog pricked up its ears and whined.
But fifty feet away a chestnut tree
with an evil blood-red face leering from a bole
was pounding up with obvious ill intent.

And the little dog said: "Don't give me up,
for I am Cerberus magicked down in size,
forced to serve the Beast for eternity,
and without me, the barriers of Hell are rent
and the hungry ghosts set free."

Picking him up, the girl leapt into the pit, and hid
behind a junction which stank of gas and super glue.
She hurriedly put on the ring.
This was a mistake as we all know now
that such rings make you visible
to demons like you know who.
With a silent shriek the awful tree
sprang into the pit, his claw-like branches seeking to grab her,
while the dog howled in helpless sympathy.

The girl hurled the brandy bottle at the bole
and used the matches for her cheroots
to set the unholy monster ablaze.
Grabbing the dog, she climbed up the side
of the noisesome pit. Once at the rim,
she lassooed a gas pipe and gave it a tug.
The Tattooed Tree went up like a bomb.
All was suddenly as bright as noon
and windows shattered all the way to Leyton Lagoon.

"Free at last !" cried Cerberus, returned
to normal size (five feet to the shoulder)
and to his three-headed splendour.
One head barked, a second howled,
and the third licked her soot-stained face.
"I'm off home to Hell with a tale to tell,
of a brave girl who trashed a wicked tree!"
But when he left her, the ring turned to worthless brass,
the magic belt became a length of old rope,
and the boots mere cheap trainers,
made by child slaves on the night shift,
in a ruined factory by the lost Aral Sea.
But glorious to say, that one night's loot
enabled her to move to Chelsea
and mix with a better class of monster,
—or so I hope.

Gingelly Poonac

I found the Devil hiding in my dusty cellar
and ordered him to get out.
"You can't do this!" he cried,
"There's really nothing left for me
out there since the Old Boy died.
Without Him I'm just a joke! —Please let me stay,
I won't be any trouble, I swear !"
A cunning look came into the Devil's dull red eyes:
"After all, you put up all those pagan gods,
and even that twister Pan who
chucked me out of Hell, isn't it true?"

"Pan was ruler there long before you,
so get out of my house! Or do I call in the boys ?"

But he would not shift, and the *"boys"*
(Castor and Pollux, Ares and Apollo)
were all engrossed in the Romania-Macedonia match.
Luckily the *"girls"* heard my angry voice
and rushed down the steps to lend a hand.
Grey-eyed Athena (my favourite)
laid him low with an uppercut,
Artemis took his feet, Aphrodite, clad only in her *lingerie*,
seized an arm and I the other.
As we bore the cursing fiend to my front door,
young Eros called : "There's a bunch of tramps outside
all demanding words with your unwanted guest."

The Father of Lies dug his claw
into the jamb, protesting all the while,
(and to this day you may see the marks in my poor door)
but we gave him the bum's rush
and out he sailed, knocking down a crowd,
including Baal, Belial and Ashtaroth, quite a crush,
all fallen on hard times and left leaderless.

Aphrodite tore bricks and concrete
from my front wall and laid into them like a Trojan,
(and to this day you can still see the gaps she made.)
The demons staggered off down Francis Road
shaking their cans of export cider
and threatening revenge. Artemis put an arrow into
Belial's arse, which speeded them all up,
and Athena, leaping on to the wall,
uttered a great *paean* which turned the sky black.
From the breast pocket of her *Olympic Airways* tunic
she fetched out her compact mirror which flashed and grew
into the great shield with the Gorgon's head,
and so turned Mammon into chalk when he glanced back.

—The remnants of the Devil's hellish regiment
were last seen living in a disused
toolshed on the allotments in Coppermill Lane,
where a scrawled sign all wonky and bent
announced *Pandaemonium* to the world.
(And my poor wall is cracked from the heat
of the Maiden's divine and lovely feet).

Athena, the warrior goddess,
grinned and said: "Never had such fun
since we last saw the Titans off."
Artemis gave me a comradely punch on the arm
and Aphrodite rewarded me with a little kiss.
We picked up the fossil Mammon
and stuck him in the garden as a sort of gnome,
but the acid rain melted him away
and he left no traces on my home.

You know I love the gods and honour them,
and pay for their *pizza* and takeaways.

But they'll never return to Olympus
with its ancient plumbing and no satellite TV,
but continue to crash with me,
which is why, Great Zeus, I am writing to you
at your retirement village in Cefalu.
Feeding a host of gods costs quite a bit,
when they wander around physically incarnate,
so as a responsible father could you chip in
with the odd contribution? Or even a regular direct debit?

Palmyra Jaggery

The broken doll in the alley marks
the entrance to Tartarus
but you must listen for the sound
of fireworks and drums
which mark the revelry of moonstruck
dossers and the alcoholic bums.
The creatures of twilight have moved out
of the railway arches at Leytonstone Midland
to escape the eternal Guy Fawkes Night
and now hang around the War Memorial
feeding half-chewed chicken nuggets to the Harpies.
The satyr who bangs at your bolted door
has stolen a jar of *brinjal* pickle and *nan* bread
from the sidestreet Asian store
and offers it in return for a place
by your fire, but the Fatso Daddy in you
wishes him away and refuses him a bed.
(So let him be taken away to a place in the hills
where the men in white and the starchy ladies can
open up his horned skull with *Black & Decker* drills.)

Fortuna hides maggots in her fashionable *chapeau*
and snores in a cardboard palace clutching a torn
lottery ticket with sixes, sevens and a thirteen:
all revealed to her by cutting the Tarot.

Babalu wears the patched clothes of the dead,
eats food rejected by others in a broken dish,
and is chased by little dogs down strange alleys,
his grimy patched shirt split open at the back,
so that all that you see is only an old black tramp
with a battered trilby on his grizzled head.
This I know because he dosses in my neighbour's shed.

No beggar is really what he seems in Leytonstone
and you have to go as far as Stratford to find one
born within the last century or completely human.
So ask the humming Tenner Lady about the glorious city
just around the corner and the swollen sun
floating above the horizon, *fata Morgana* on a crest
being a station on the Central Line in Epping Forest.

The Door to Tartarus

That bag-lady pushing a wonky pram
is Hecate and around her throat hangs
a crude whistle of white curlew bone
made by a Stone Age hunter.
Now it calls her mangey alley cats
back to their cardboard home.
But you need guts to ask her.

So look instead for a shifty stranger
whistling an ancient tune,
wearing something dark at night,
a moth-eaten cap hiding his horns,
and approach *him* for directions.

"There is a door drawn in superglue
on the wall of the Turkish
mini-market and ghosts
and goblins pass through.
Watch out for the wicked trolls
under the railway arches
who steal babies and pay no rent.
—*And* witches writing a children's classic
in the laundromat whilst
their knickers, like a pastel tent
do the light fantastic."

This I heard from great Pan's lips,
sitting in the bus-shelter
opposite my house,
waiting for the last W14,
on his left a drunken South African
chewing on *biltong* strips,
my vixen and three cubs
watching with interest on the kerb,
and on his right, ibis-headed Thoth.

The sozzled Piet from Jo'burg
must have tried it for I never
saw him again: Thoth, I know,
took over an undertaker's
in Wanstead, but never made it go.

The Life and Times
of KAWPZ of Leytonstone

Once you could walk into the forest
and talk with the bears,
when time was optional
before the clocks melted and ran
like fondant marzipan,
before the snakes in the walls
made us afraid to look in mirrors.
Now the Beast Boy writes His name
all over the High Street,
calling himself KAWPZ,
which added up reduces to the number
777.
He creates stars out of orgasm
to shine in splintered glory upon
Himself from the glass of shop-fronts
where the bullets strike poison fangs,
and seeks to multiply little *kawpzes*
in our gutters like toads engendered from rocks.
He rules all the crack tract
between the *Green Man*
and Elizabeth's Hunting Lodge
and is less approachable
than the bears.

The Waters of Noon

Just ask me, and I will come and get you,
Japanese girl on the tube, stretching across the aisle
to read the map: a young willow bendy
and all bendy, and show you a good time
in the *Kentucky Fried Chicken* across
from the Methodist Church where the bullet
holes are still visible from last month's
drive-by drugs shooting. This is our local
portal for bad girls who lick the posters
of pop stars, shout down alleyways really
loud, eager to jump through plate-glass windows
to land in *Purth Lludd*, the Ludgate temple
beneath St. Paul's where paedophiles in black
cannot find them.
Let me tell your fortune.
I can read the future in the *Fanta*
rings on the greasy formica, or throw
your chicken bones on the tiled but unwashed
floor, but you prefer the cards: I see
(coming soon) a homeward journey beyond
the Lightning-Struck Twin Towers of New York
and on to the Land of Smiles, all those miles,
under the Sun, ruled by the Moon, alone,
you, filled with Starborn reminiscences:
perhaps about one you did not avoid—
the Page of Swords, young Jimmy, our fourteen-
year-old crack dealer, screaming threats on
his mobile, scared only of his mother,
the Queen of Cups, always in her cups, whom
he fed with fags and Belgian chocolate.
You can still see some of his blood staining
the pavement just over there: look, here's Death
escorting him to the Devil. Another
tourist!—but one who can't keep away from

43

the smokers, jokers, grinning child-chokers
of the Coronation Gardens, where now
the bad girls go to connect. No more do
I see, but that's enough of Jimmy for
our today, tomorrow and for all time.

The Pillars of the Temple

The pillars of the temple have fallen:
only the legends remain woven from nightmares,
written with spidery writing in leather tomes
under Latin titles, ascribed to Cornelius Agrippa;
decorated with lots of pentagrams,
and spells which ring out of rocks
and make lizards leap.

One day you will take the 66 to Romford,
but it will become the 666
at Gants Hill, racing down
a cratered highway between
burnt-out tenements,
and the only music on the radio
will be Polish rap. Then you will know
that at your house an unknown face
peers out the uncleaned front windows,
and that you will not be missed.

The Hills and Valleys
of *Poundland*, Romford

You may enter at the front,
but never exit by that door:
for the needle of the compass
spins round like a whirligig,
and does your head in.
You will join others lost on the floor,
perhaps the grunting Australopithecines,
and fight them for scraps of antelope liver,
surviving because you are bigger
and more desperate. If you are lucky,
you may find the last Roman Legion
and march off in search of the Isles of the Blest,
but still find yourself two thousand years earlier
on a boat bearing quarried stone blocks from Aswan
to holy Heliopolis and its vast and busy docks.
The only protection from such
time-slips is to repeat the mantra:
"I will spend more than one pound"
and the visions pressing down
on you from the sun-blasted rocks,
or the mosquito-infested jungles
where the drums beat on and on,
will fade so that you may at last stumble
down one side of the great waterfall,
where the earth ends and collapse
exhausted in some other *Poundland*
perhaps in the Euro or dollar zone,
perhaps in some place where
educated dinosaurs rule a
benign galactic empire and cannot
quote an exchange rate for you alone.

Area of Development

Like wrestlers we roll in the dust naked,
our white arms squeezing the breath from our throats.
our ears possessed by the passionate notes
of the pneumatic drills. Our lips are caked
with the dry dung of demolished sunbaked
bricks, a river of ground sand like silk floats
between our lascivious toes and coats
your thigh with maps of kisses still unstaked
by speculation. Taste the memories
spent among the peeling papers of these
ransacked rooms, and the ammoniac beds
with grease stains budding beneath heads
racked with unwashed ecstasies on grey sheets—
stains of summer on walls above these streets.

East End Haiku

The bus speeds past late,
full of faces from hell—but
not stopping, thank God!

Beating up his wife,
his shirt rose, his pants slipped down,
exposing his arse.

Climbing tube steps I
see my shadow. Coming down
nothing but shadows.

Motorway bridge lights
shimmer on the black tarmac.
Who is buried there?

Printed in the United States
43721LVS00006B/775